FOCUS
on Spelling

G000293191

Spelling

Book 4

**Joyce Sweeney and
Carol Doncaster**

Using this book

This book will help you to develop good spelling strategies that you can use in your writing.

What's in a unit

Each unit is set out in the same way as the example here.

Unit heading
This tells you what you will be learning about.

Focus
This helps you think about the spelling rule.

More to think about
Activities to practise and develop your understanding.

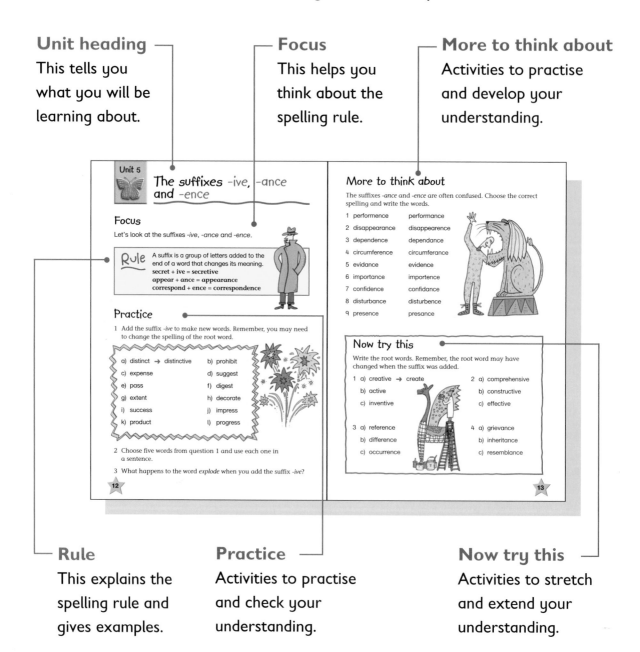

Rule
This explains the spelling rule and gives examples.

Practice
Activities to practise and check your understanding.

Now try this
Activities to stretch and extend your understanding.

Contents

Unstressed vowels in multisyllable words

Focus

Which is the unstressed vowel in words like *teacher* or *camera*?

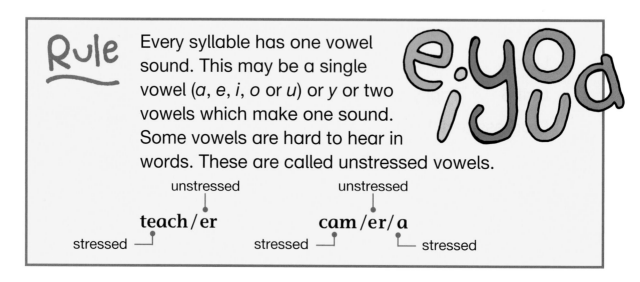

Rule Every syllable has one vowel
sound. This may be a single
vowel (*a, e, i, o* or *u*) or *y* or two
vowels which make one sound.
Some vowels are hard to hear in
words. These are called unstressed vowels.

unstressed

teach/er

stressed

unstressed

cam/er/a

stressed   stressed

Practice

Write the words. Mark out the syllables.
Circle the unstressed vowel in each word.

1 vegetable → veg/ⓔ/ta/ble

2 temperature   3 seven

4 button   5 sister

6 pedal   7 husband

8 pupil   9 happening

10 interest   11 excellent

12 quarrel   13 external

More to think about

Each word below is missing an unstressed vowel. Write the words correctly. Then underline the unstressed vowel.

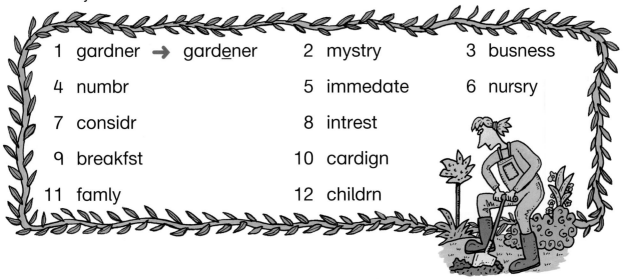

1 gardner → gard<u>e</u>ner   2 mystry   3 busness

4 numbr   5 immedate   6 nursry

7 considr   8 intrest

9 breakfst   10 cardign

11 famly   12 childrn

Now try this

Two vowels coming together often make one sound, for example *rain*. However, sometimes when two vowels come together they make two sounds, for example *dial*. If you say the word slowly, pronouncing each vowel, it is easier to hear the unstressed vowel.

1 Write the words. Mark the syllables. Circle the unstressed vowel.

   a) diamond → di/ⓐ/mond

   b) violent   c) medium

   d) familiar   e) cruel   f) fuel

   g) poem   h) valuable   i) obedient

   j) casual   k) fluoride   l) sanctuary

2 Choose three words from question 1 and use each in a sentence.

Prefixes from other languages

Focus

Did you know that some prefixes in the English language come from other languages?

 The English language has been added to by many ancient languages. Understanding the origin of words can help you to understand their meaning.

Practice

Latin has influenced the English language.

Prefix	Meaning	From it we get ...
aqua-	water	aquarium
audi-	hear	auditorium
super-	above/greater	supersonic
trans-	across/through/beyond	transport

Use a dictionary to find at least two words for each prefix.

Prefix	Word	Meaning
aqua-	aquarium	a glass fish tank
audi-		
super-		
trans-		

More to think about

Ancient Greek has influenced the English language.

Prefix	Greek word	Meaning	From it we get ...
aero-	*aer*	air	aeroplane
micro-	*mikros*	small	microphone
tele-	*tele*	far	telegraph

1 Use a dictionary to find at least three words for each prefix.

Prefix	Word	Meaning
aero-	aeroplane	a flying vehicle
micro-		
tele-		

2 Choose three words from above, each with a different prefix, and write a sentence for each.

Now try this

1 What do the words below mean?
  Check your answers in the dictionary.

  a) octopus ➔ an eight-legged sea creature

  b) binoculars   c) octahedron   d) bikini

  e) bilingual   f) octagon   g) binary

2 The prefixes *oct-* and *bi-* are both prefixes from the Ancient World. What else do these prefixes have in common?

3 Find two more examples of prefixes that indicate numbers.

Suffixes as a support for spelling

Focus

What is a suffix? What does it do? Let's look at some common suffixes.

 Rule A suffix is a group of letters added to the end of a word that changes its meaning.
visit + or = visitor

Practice

1 Add a suffix from the boxes to the words in the list below to make new words. You can use a suffix more than once. Check the new words in a dictionary.

-ism	-let	-like	-wise	-or

-wards	-er	-ish	-some

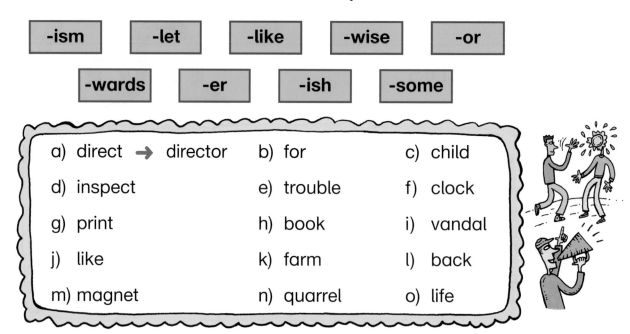

a) direct → director   b) for   c) child

d) inspect   e) trouble   f) clock

g) print   h) book   i) vandal

j) like   k) farm   l) back

m) magnet   n) quarrel   o) life

2 Choose nine words from those above, one for each suffix. Write a definition for each of the nine words.

More to think about

1 Add two different suffixes to the words in the table to
make new words.

Root word	+ Suffix 1	+ Suffix 2		Useful suffixes
enjoy				-ment
instruct				-ing
act				-ed
hope				-tion
race				-or
friend				-fully
hand				-ly
like				-less
				-ship
				-ness

2 Make a list of other suffixes that you know. Can any of them
be added to the words above?

Now try this

Choose one set of three words from those in question 1 above.
Write a sentence for each word.

The suffixes -ary, -ery and -ory

Focus

Let's look at the suffixes *-ary*, *-ery* and *-ory*.

 Rule The suffixes *-ery*, *-ory* and *-ary* can sound very similar and are often confused. Always check your spelling of words using these suffixes if you are not sure.

Practice

Add the suffix *-ery* to the root words to make new words. You may need to change the spelling of the root word. Check your answers in a dictionary.

Root word	Root word + *-ery*	Root word	Root word + *-ery*
nurse	nursery	rob	
jewel		slip	
bribe		cook	
join		bake	
brew		machine	
scene		pot	
brave		slave	

More to think about

1 Write the words. Each word ends in *-ary* or *-ory*.
   Check your answers in a dictionary.

a) l_____   b) f_____   c) c_____

d) d_____   e) s_____   f) F_____

2 Work out the answers to these clues. Each word ends in *-ary* or
   -ory. Check your answers in a dictionary.

a) a radio or television programme giving
   information about real people and events   d_____

b) the study of the past   h_____

Now try this

1 These words end in *-ary*, *-ery* or *-ory*. Some of them have
   been spelled wrongly. Write the misspelled words correctly.

   cookery   delivary   sanctuary   ordinery   necessery

   secretery   granary   tributory   anniversory   laboratory

2 Choose five words from question 1 and write a sentence
   for each one.

The suffixes -ive, -ance and -ence

Focus

Let's look at the suffixes *-ive*, *-ance* and *-ence*.

Rule A suffix is a group of letters added to the end of a word that changes its meaning.

secret + ive = secretive

appear + ance = appearance

correspond + ence = correspondence

Practice

1 Add the suffix *-ive* to make new words. Remember, you may need to change the spelling of the root word.

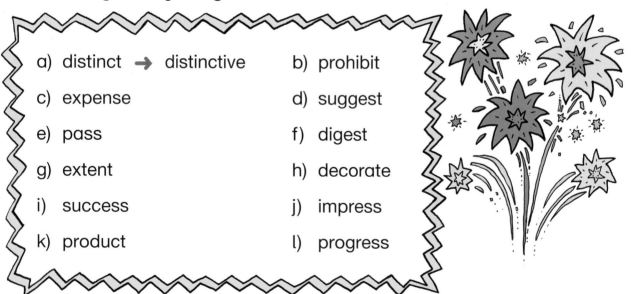

a) distinct → distinctive   b) prohibit

c) expense   d) suggest

e) pass   f) digest

g) extent   h) decorate

i) success   j) impress

k) product   l) progress

2 Choose five words from question 1 and use each one in a sentence.

3 What happens to the word *explode* when you add the suffix *-ive*?

More to think about

The suffixes *-ance* and *-ence* are often confused. Choose the correct spelling and write the words.

1 performence   performance
2 disappearance   disappearence
3 dependence   dependance
4 circumference   circumferance
5 evidance   evidence
6 importance   importence
7 confidence   confidance
8 disturbance   disturbence
9 presence   presance

Now try this

Write the root words. Remember, the root word may have changed when the suffix was added.

1 a) creative → create
   b) active
   c) inventive

2 a) comprehensive
   b) constructive
   c) effective

3 a) reference
   b) difference
   c) occurrence

4 a) grievance
   b) inheritance
   c) resemblance

Tricky words 1

Focus

Can you think of ways to remember how to spell tricky words like *aerial*?

  A mnemonic is a way of remembering the spelling of a tricky word.

aerial **a**ngry
elephants
ride
in
amber
lorries

Sometimes it helps you to remember how to spell a word if you can picture the mnemonic.

Practice

1 Write the words. Underline the part of the word that the mnemonic helps you to remember how to spell.

   a) <u>is</u>land   An island is land.

   b) separate   There is a rat in separate.

   c) believe   Don't believe a lie.

   d) soldiers   Soldiers sometimes die.

2 Funny mnemonics that you make up yourself are often the easiest to remember. Make up mnemonics for these tricky words.

   a) tongue   b) cough   c) amateur   d) previous

More to think about

Sometimes a rhyme or a mnemonic can help you to remember the spellings of tricky words.

difficulty Mr **D**, Mr **I**
Mr **FFI**,
Mr **C**, Mr **U**
Mr **LTY**!

rhythm **r**hythm
has
your
toes
hopping
madly

Make up a rhyme or a mnemonic to help you remember these tricky words.

1 elephant   2 beautiful   3 friend

4 because   5 guest   6 necessary

Now try this

The following strategies will help you to spell tricky words.

- pronouncing silent letters:
  for scissors say **s - c - issors**
- exaggerating syllables: **ab - so - lute - ly**
- finding words within words: **colourful**

What strategy would you use to help you remember these tricky words?

1 lieutenant   2 conscience   3 abscess

4 quarantine   5 definite   6 discipline

7 rhubarb   8 meringue   9 vicious

Progress test 1

A Write the words. Circle the unstressed vowels.

1 traveller   2 peculiar   3 reasonable   4 difference

5 temporary   6 sickening   7 miserable   8 discovery

9 unusual   10 diary   11 separate   12 reference

B Add a prefix to make a new word each time.

| aero- | trans- | super- | tele- |
| bi- | micro- | aqua- |

1 _____scope

2 _____natural

3 _____vise

4 _____atlantic

5 _____dynamic

6 _____chip

7 _____lung

8 _____monthly

9 _____wave

10 _____space

11 _____text

12 _____tic

C Add a suffix to each word to make new words. Remember, you may need to change the root word.

1 trouble   2 child   3 clock   4 after
5 book   6 respect   7 bake   8 educate
9 journal   10 buy   11 back   12 quarrel

D Rewrite the sentences, spelling the underlined words correctly.

1 The woman wore sparkling <u>jewellory</u>.

2 The couple celebrated their <u>anniversery</u>.

3 The <u>secretery</u> typed very quickly.

4 She checked the spelling in a <u>dictionery</u>.

5 Scamp was no <u>ordinery</u> dog.

6 He rushed off to the <u>laboratery</u>.

7 The new car was <u>extraordinery</u>.

8 They ate their lunch in the <u>refectary</u>.

9 The umbrella was <u>necessery</u> as it was raining.

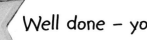

Well done – you've finished your progress test.

Tricky words 2

Focus

Can you think of more ways to remember how to spell tricky words like *necessary*?

> **Rule**
>
> Here are some different strategies to help you remember tricky spellings.
>
> - Say the word slowly and exaggerate the pronunciation.
> - Use the "Look, Say, Cover, Write, Check" method.
> - Look for smaller words within big words.
> - Make up your own mnemonics.
> - Always use a dictionary to check.

Practice

1 Write the correct spellings. Think of a strategy to help you remember the correct one.

a) embarassed	embarrased	embarrassed ✔
b) necessery	necessary	neccesary
c) parallel	parralel	parrallel
d) acommodation	accommodation	accomodation
e) possesses	posesses	posseses
f) occasional	ocassional	occassional

2 Use each correctly spelled word in a sentence.

More to think about

The words below can be difficult to spell. Saying the words slowly and exaggerating the pronunciation will help you. Write the words. Mark the syllables. Underline the unstressed vowels.

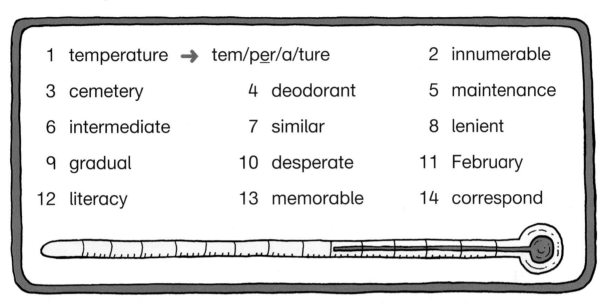

1 temperature → tem/p<u>e</u>r/a/ture

2 innumerable

3 cemetery

4 deodorant

5 maintenance

6 intermediate

7 similar

8 lenient

9 gradual

10 desperate

11 February

12 literacy

13 memorable

14 correspond

Now try this

A mnemonic is a way of remembering the spelling of tricky words, like this:

● *Because*: **B**ig **e**lephants **c**an't **a**lways **u**se **s**mall **e**xits.

1 Invent a mnemonic to help you remember the spelling of each of these words.

a) biscuit   b) definite   c) hygiene

d) excellent   e) friend   f) percentage

2 Now illustrate one of your mnemonics.

Words from other languages 1

Focus

Why do the letters *ch* make different sounds in the words *chaos* and *chute*?

> **Rule**
>
> In words that come from the Greek language, the letters *ch* can make the sound *k*.
>
> **mechanical   chaos   stomach**
>
> In words that come from the French language, the letters *ch* can make the sound *sh*.
>
> **chute**

Practice

1 Write the words.

a)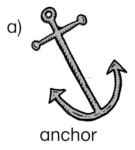

anchor

b)

c)

d)

2 Work out the answers to these clues. Check your answers in a dictionary.

a) a group of people who play musical instruments together

_____ch_____

b) a state of complete disorder

ch_____

c) the fictional people in a film, play or book

ch_____

More to think about

1 Write out the answers to these clues.
  Check your answers in a dictionary.

  a) a wooden house with a sloping roof, in a
     mountain area or a holiday camp   ch_____

  b) a leaflet which gives information about
     products or services   _____ch_____

2 Write the words.

  a)    b) 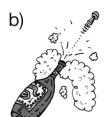   c)    d)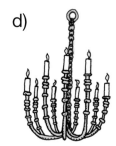

Now try this

Use *ch, c* or *sh* to complete the words. Write the sentences.

1 The accident at the traffi__c__ lights __aused __aos.

2 At __ristmas the __ildren sang __arols in the __athedral.

3 The __alendar dates are arranged in __ronological order.

4 The __over for the ma__ine is on the __elf.

5 Mi__elle __owed us how to play __arades.

Words from other languages 2

Focus

Why do the letters *ph* make the sound *f* in words like *physics*?

$R\upsilon le$ In words that come from the Greek language, the letters *ph* make the sound *f*.

physics   **ph**rase   **ph**oenix

Practice

1 Write the words.

a)

alphabet

b)

c)

d)

e)

f)

2 Work out the answers to these clues. Each word has the letters *ph* in it. Check your answers in a dictionary.

a) a punctuation mark used to join words together   hy_____

b) a mythical bird   _____n__x

c) words on a tomb about a person who has died   epi_____

d) a mythical monster with a lion's body and a
   human head   s_____nx

More to think about

Add a word containing *ph* to the word families below.

1 clarinet   trombone   sa___ph____

2 cousin   niece   n__ph____

3 giraffe   rhinoceros   e____ph___

4 biology   chemistry   phy_____

5 comma   full stop   apo_____ph__

6 cube   triangular prism   sph_____

Now try this

photo	graph	auto	tele

	copier	graphy	copy	grapher

1 Join two boxes to make seven more words.
   You can use each box more than once.

   photo + grapher = photographer

2 Some of the new words belong to
   the same word family. How many
   word families can you find?
   Write the words in family groups.

Tricky words 3

Focus

Can you think of ways to remember how to spell tricky words like *advice* and *advise*?

>
> **The text around the word indicates the correct spelling.**
> **I need some good *advice*.**
> **I would *advise* you to go to the doctor.**

Practice

advice is a noun	*advise* is a verb
practice is a noun	*practise* is a verb

Remember: *ice* is a noun – and *advice* and *practice* are nouns, too. Complete the sentences using *advice*, *advise*, *practice* or *practise*.

1 The brass band was told it needed to <u>*practise*</u>.

2 I left the house early on your _____.

3 The dental _____ is closed at the weekend.

4 The lawyer will _____ her client on his defence.

5 Cleaning your teeth after every meal is good _____.

6 Louise should _____ every night before the competition.

7 The teacher gave the students good _____ on how to study.

8 I would _____ you not to drive in these treacherous conditions.

More to think about

altar is a noun   to *alter* is a verb

These words are sometimes confused.
Using different strategies, like the following one,
will help you to remember how to spell them.

An altar is a raised table in a church.
Altar has *ta* in it for *table*.

Think of some strategies to help you remember how to spell
these words.

1 stationary/stationery

2 lose/loose

3 course/coarse

4 council/counsel

Now try this

council/counsel	altar/alter	coarse/course
stationary/stationery	lose/loose	

Complete the sentences using the words above.

1 The joiner used _____ sandpaper to smooth the wood.

2 The dressmaker will _____ the length of my coat.

3 The student wore _____ clothing for karate.

4 The local _____ met to discuss vandalism.

5 The runaway lorry hit a _____ bus.

Spelling rules 1

Focus

What other spelling rules are useful to learn?

Rule

- *q* is always followed by *u* in the English language

- *ti* and *ci* are the two spellings most frequently used to say *sh* within a word

- *si* is used when the *sh* sound is voiced: **division**

- *cede*, *ceed* and *sede* are easily confused, but *cede* is used most often at the end of a word: pre**cede**

Practice

1 The words below can be tricky to remember. Use the "Look, Say, Cover, Write, Check" method to learn how to spell them.

a) quite   b) quiet   c) quench

d) quadrilateral   e) qualification   f) quaver

g) quay   h) query   i) queue

j) quiche   k) quotation   l) questionnaire

2 Choose two words from question 1 and think of a mnemonic for each one.

3 Choose two more words from question 1 with more than one syllable and mark out the syllables.

More to think about

1 Complete the words using *ti, ci* or *si*.

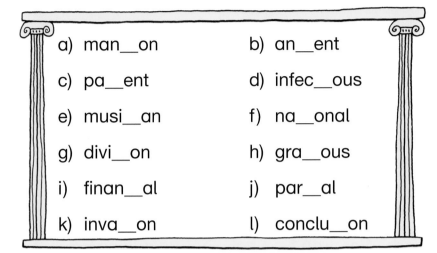

a) man__on

b) an__ent

c) pa__ent

d) infec__ous

e) musi__an

f) na__onal

g) divi__on

h) gra__ous

i) finan__al

j) par__al

k) inva__on

l) conclu__on

2 Write out the words that contain the letters *ti* again.
Mark the syllables.

Now try this

1 The letter strings *cede, ceed* and *sede* are often confused.
Complete and learn this rule to help you to remember
which to use.

The three *ceed* words are: suc<u>ceed</u>   ex_____   pro_____

The one *sede* word is: super_____

All other words use *cede*: pre_____   re_____

2 Use a dictionary to check the
meanings of these words.
Choose three words and write
a sentence for each.

Spelling rules 2

Focus

What should you remember when you add a suffix to a root word?

Rule

If a word ends in a consonant + *y*, change the *y* to *i* before adding a suffix, except for *-ing*.

cry → **cried** → **crying**

If a word ends in *e*, drop the final *e* before adding a vowel suffix (like *-ing* or *-ed*) or *y*, but keep the *e* before adding a consonant suffix (like *-ly* or *-ness*).

late → **lately** → **lateness**

If a word ends in a single *l* after a short vowel, double the *l* before adding the suffix.

signal → **signalling**

Practice

1 Add as many suffixes from the boxes as you can to each word to make new words.

-ing   **-y**   **-ly**   **-able**

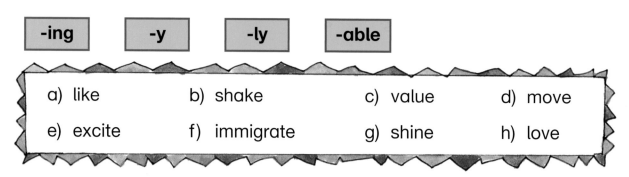

| a) like | b) shake | c) value | d) move |
| e) excite | f) immigrate | g) shine | h) love |

2 Add *-able* to the words below to make new words.

a) replace   b) notice   c) charge   d) manage

More to think about

Add as many suffixes as you can to each word to make new words. You will not be able to add all the suffixes to each word.

| -es | -ness | -ed | -ly | -er | -ing |

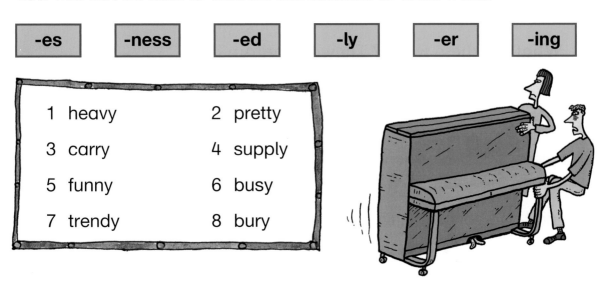

1 heavy 2 pretty

3 carry 4 supply

5 funny 6 busy

7 trendy 8 bury

Now try this

1 Add the suffix to the root words.

a) signal stencil tunnel **-ing** → signalling

b) panel pedal cancel **-ed**

2 Choose one suffix to add to each word.

| -ic | -ist | -er |

a) medal b) metal c) travel

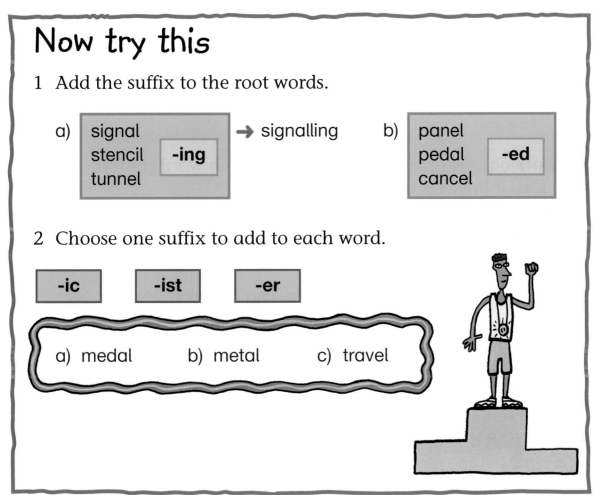

Progress test 2

A What are these words? They all contain *ch.*

1 arranged in the order in which things happen   ch_____

2 a state of disorder   ch_____

3 a piece of fabric attached to a person to allow
   them to fall safely from an aircraft   ____ch_____

4 a part of a song which is repeated after each verse ch_____

5 a large group of musicians   ____ch_____

6 a sparkling white wine made in France   ch_____

7 reflection of sound   ____ch_____

8 a booklet that gives information about a product
   or service   ____ch_____

B Work out the answers to these clues. Each word contains *ph.*
Check your answers in a dictionary.

1 a machine which makes instant copies   ph_____

2 the 26 letters from A to Z   ____ph_____

3 words on a tomb about the person who has died   _____ph

4 the signature of a famous person   _____ph

5 a great fear or hatred of something   ph_____

6 a chart showing number information   _____ph

7 your sister's or brother's son   ____ph_____

8 a large long-tailed game bird   ph_____

C Add a suffix to make a new word each time. You may need to drop a letter or double a letter before adding the suffix.

-ure	-ive	-ance	-ence

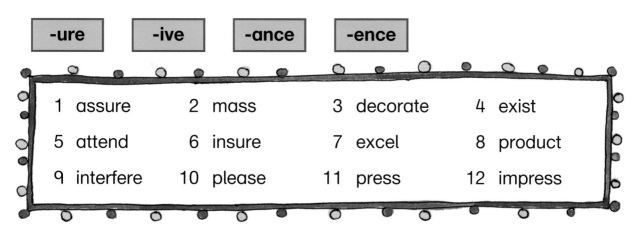

1 assure	2 mass	3 decorate	4 exist
5 attend	6 insure	7 excel	8 product
9 interfere	10 please	11 press	12 impress

D Complete the sentences.

1 I need to _____ every day before the competition.
(practice/practise)

2 My sister is about to _____ her first tooth.
(loose/lose)

3 The coach will _____ the pupils about the best running shoes to buy.
(advise/advice)

4 Chicken was served as the main _____.
(coarse/course)

5 Paper, pens and other writing equipment are called _____.
(stationary/stationery)

6 The drought had a disastrous _____ on the people.
(affect/effect)

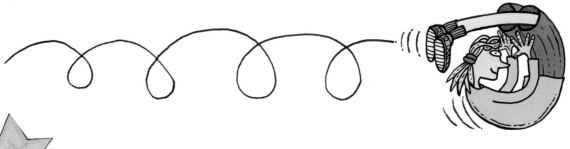

Well done – you've finished your progress test.

Spellchecker

Write the signs correctly. Check the spellings in your dictionary.

1 Broshure of ..... *speciality orcids*

2 **Documentery** *Vandlism –* the way forward

3 *Jewelry Sail*

4 Charlie's Sircus Daily Performences

5 **Airobatic Display** *10 a.m.*

6 *Fieldway + farmacy +*

7 **Williamswell Practise** Surjery Hours

8 Next parashute jump 2 p.m.

9 **quew hear for tikkets**

10 *Favourible intrest rates*

11 **Bransfield Counsel Comittee Meating Room 7**

Well done – you've finished your Spellchecker.